Ritual Magic for Beginners

Basics, Elements, Applications and Examples

Contact: www.HarryEilenstein.de
Harry.Eilenstein@web.de
Harry Eilenstein at youtube

Production and publishing house: BoD – Books on Demand, Norderstedt

ISBN: 9783754302385

Table of Contents

I What is a Ritual?

In terms of form, a ritual is an action fixed in its course. This broad definition also includes putting one's children to bed in the evening, which always follows the same pattern to make it easier for both parents and children. The course of a federal election is also a ritual in this sense.

However, rituals can also be narrowed down by their subject matter. This book is about rituals used in magic – although there is a smooth transition from magic to meditation if you have a closer look at rituals. For example, both use certain traditional "power words" that have a magical effect: Spell-formulas in magic and mantras in meditation.

In terms of content, a magic ritual is an action that one performs in order to achieve a magical effect. Since magic is the effecting of a material change caused directly by consciousness, it is obviously not the ritual action itself that produces the magical effect. Consequently, the magical action, i.e. the ritual, is an aid to concentration and imagination for the magician.

This interpretation is also confirmed by the fact that rituals change over time and experienced magicians use less and less rituals and the words, gestures and actions needed for magic become less and less – the experienced magician does not need these aids so much. This does not mean that rituals are superfluous – with increasing experience one merely needs this tool less often.

The previous definition of a "magic ritual" also makes it possible to distinguish this form of ritual from similar "standardized actions". For example, the cult consists of a larger number of rituals, which all belong to certain contexts such as sowing, vision quest, wedding, burial, chieftain election, temple consecration, and so on.

Within a cult, it is possible that a magical effect is also attributed to the individual ritual, or that it is performed because of a hoped-for magical effect, but this is not the essential point. The aim of the cult is primarily the maintenance of the right order.

Another term that bears resemblance to "ritual" is "ceremony." It, too, refers to a traditional, regulated course of action. "Ceremony," however, has a more pompous sound than "ritual," and the association with magic is not as pronounced. Ceremonies belong more to cult – rituals more to magic. This is not a sharp definition, however, but rather a different emphasis.

Since a ritual is a "formally planned and usually often repeated action", the play in theatres would also be a ritual. The first plays in Greece actually originated from mystery plays, i.e. from rituals that depicted stories from the life of the gods. They were also expected to have a purifying effect on the spectators. They were intended as a stimulus for self-reflection and self-discovery. The play, however, has increasingly developed into a means of entertaining the spectators or instructing them. In more recent times, drama is increasingly intended to appeal to the feelings and intellect of the audience, but no longer primarily to their innermost being, their soul.

The definition of a ritual as a "formally fixed action" also fits just about all plays. If you trace back the history of games, you will eventually also come across magical rituals, although these have largely become cult.

For example, the dice games derive from the Germanic dice oracle, "chess" and "checkers" from the 8·8 field overview of the 64 hexagrams of the I Ching; the "goose game" and like games from the ancient Egyptian Senet, which represented the otherworld path; soccer, tennis, badminton, field hockey, cricket, rugby, etc., on the one hand from the Germanic ball game, and on the other hand from the Central American oracle game, by which human sacrifice was determined; etc.

- - -

The origin of rituals lies in the Neolithic period. At that time, agriculture and animal husbandry made it possible for 500 times more people to live together than before in the Paleolithic, when people had lived in groups of up to a maximum of 30 people, who lived by hunting and gathering. As a result, the previous Paleolithic principle of association was no longer sufficient to be able to have an overview – association requires getting to know each individual person.

Therefore the analogy was invented: the comparison. This led to more abstract terms that referred to a certain structure or property, such as "carpenter", "black-smith", "sowing date", "harvest" and the like. Thus, analogy series emerged: "All blacksmiths are strong." In this way, complex archetypes developed, which had a certain quality and dynamics. These were the gods: the Great Mother, the Grain God, the Wilderness God, the Earth God, the Primordial Man or Ancestor, the Goddess of the World Tree, the God of the Ritual Potion, the God of the Straight Axis of the Potter's Wheel, and so on.

There was also the temporal analogy: the annual circle. In this circle the same activities and rituals or festivals were repeated every year. The maintenance of the order, which had proved to be the most effective so far, gave rise to the orientation to tradition. The totality of these deities, cycles and rituals resulted in the archetype of right behavior: mythology.

The observance of the right order was the central element of Neolithic behavior. The "rightness" that was thereby maintained is the central concept. It is found in all magical-mythological worldviews. It has a lot of different names, that all descibe this rightness and its effect on people.

Egyptians:	ma'at	("mother")
Sumerians:	me	("mother")
Teutons:	sidr	("ancient way")
Chinese:	tao	("way")
Tibetans:	tashi	("happy destiny")
Navahos:	ho'zhong	("beauty")
Romans:	ritus	("wheel")
Hittites:	aya	("wheel")
Indians (old):	rita	("wheel")
Persians:	asha	("wheel")
Indians (new):	dharma	("poetic metre")
Celts:	fhirinne	("truth")
Slavs:	prawda	("truth")
Greeks:	dikaios	("justice")
etc.		

The different names show the quality of the rightness:

The "rules of the life force" are the "roots of truth".

They are the rightness to which behavior is related in the proven, time-honored way and which creates righteousness.

It is the right measure and also the verse measure that gives rise to beauty. It is perfectly round and balanced like a wheel.

It is the gift of the Mother Goddess that helps to go one's own way and find a happy destiny.

The word "ritual" shows that its origin lies in the idea of an action repeated at regular intervals at always the same point in the annual cycle: "ritual" derives from the Latin "rota" for "wheel".

- - -

At first sight, rituals differ very clearly in different cultures, religions and traditions. However, if we look at the content, structure and dynamics of rituals, we see that rituals follow an internal logic – more precisely, follow two forms of logic: on the one hand, the logic of the theme of the ritual (sowing, wedding, consecration, blessing, etc.) and, on the other hand, the logic of the action of the ritual (opening, connection with gods, transformation, ending).

For example, a blessing in all religions consists of the priest connecting with a deity and then allowing the power or consciousness of that deity to flow through himself to the blessed.

- - -

It can be useful to look at tried rituals to see what a ritual should look like in order to have an reliable magical effect.

II The Structure of a Ritual

In the construction of an effective, efficient ritual, several questions arise which one should answer oneself in approximately the order listed below.

II 1. The Aim

The first question to ask when constructing an effective ritual is the question of the aim. Without a clearly defined aim, there is no clear direction, nor is there a clear and great effect. Even if the aim is just curiosity about what can happen when performing a certain ritual, this aim should be clear.

II 2. The Motivation

When one performs a ritual, one intends to have a (magical) effect. So it is not a wrong investment of time and effort to sit down and take a good look at whether what you are aiming at as a goal is exactly what you really want.

- Is this goal only something you want to achieve so that you can do and achieve something else?

- Is the goal an extreme like addiction or asceticism, like power or powerlessness, like the desire for recognition or a hiden shame?

- Is the goal an undistorted self-expression that originates directly from the heart chakra? Does the goal arise from the experience of abundance, power and self-love? Or does it arise from the experience of lack, violence, and self-doubt?

- Is the goal in harmony with the other goals one has?

- Is the goal in harmony with what one really wants?

- Is the goal consistent with one's vision of one's own life?

The key question is:

> - Is the goal a "Yes, but …" desire or is it a "Yes, gladly!" desire? In the first case, one should fathom and reformulate the goal until it has become a "Yes, gladly!" desire. Contradictions in motivation will also show up in the effect of the ritual …

You don't have to ask yourself exactly these questions, but taking a little time to examine your own motivation might now and then have the advantage that you don't run off in the wrong direction with all your might.

You can also take a look at how great the need behind this motivation is – the more intense the motivation, the greater the effect of the ritual will probably be.

II 3. The Center

Once the goal has been formulated, reviewed, and possibly reformulated again, one can look at what the central process is in the ideas developed so far about the planned ritual. This central process will be a change, a transformation, a reinforcement – because if after the ritual everything should still be the same as before the ritual, you may as well leave the ritual undone (unless one wants to secure an existing condition by the ritual).

The goal is in the distance and in the future. What is the essential step that brings you to this goal?

This step obviously depends on the goal. Examples for the central element in a ritual can be the most different things. Strictly speaking, one should even distinguish three things: the goal, the way there and the "vehicle", i.e. the aid on this way.

> For example, if one has realized that one lives in poverty and wants to change this, prosperity is the goal. The way there can be a money spell. Then, for example, an invocation to Jupiter would be a possible aid.

> One may also come to the conclusion that the way to prosperity is the dissolution of one's own fear of poverty. The tool could then be a connection to Mother Earth.

> It would also be conceivable that in connection with the poverty theme the person has found in himself an addict and an ascetic. Then the dissolution of these two images would be the aid.

It is also possible that the magician comes to the conclusion that he does not care about all inner and outer circumstances and that he simply wants money. In this case, sigil magic would be suitable as a method, by which a wish is sent out – in this context, this wish could also be called a "magical command to life".

Several basic things come into question as the center of the ritual:

1. the establishment of a connection:
    - obtaining contact with one's own power animal, one's own power plant, and one's own power stone
        - the attainment of contact with one's own soul
        - achieving the connection to a deity
        - the attainment of the connection to the Unity/God

2. the widening of one's own consciousness (largely identical with point 1.):
        - to the realm of the psyche, power animals, elemental beings, etc.
        - to the realm of souls, spirits, angels, etc.
        - to the realm of gods, archangels etc.
        - to the realm of oneness, God, Samadhi etc.

3. the dissolution of a polarized, suffering-creating opposition:
        - the dissolving of the polarized opposition of ideal and shadow in one's own psyche:
                - addict and ascetic
                - perpetrator and victim
                - star and fan
        - dissolving the polarized opposition of ideal and shadow in a community, culture, religion, etc.

4. the establishment of a free flow of life force:
        - Kundalini ("earth-fire")
        - Bindhu ("sky-light")

5. the demarcation and defense against something:
        - general or special protection against attacks from people
        - general or special protection against attacks of "spirits"

Certainly other central dynamics can be found in a ritual. For example, the damage spells have a destruction as a goal, other forms of magic have e.g. dominance over others, the creation of dependencies and the like as a goal. You could also group rain spells and the like in a separate category.

After reviewing the goal and clarifying the motivation, one can now select the appropriate central element that will then shape the design and dynamics of the entire ritual.

II 4. The Style

This point is more important than it seems at first sight. If one performs the ritual in a style with which one is not comfortable, one will not be able to direct all one's concentration and imagination to that ritual.

For example, if one is a committed Christian and is invoking Pan in a witchcraft coven, one will inevitably have to think of the devil and become internally conflicted – which will effectively hinder the ritual.

This is true even for individual motifs: if for some participants in a ritual, for example, the snake is the symbol of the devil and for others it is a symbol of Kundalini, there could be difficulties …

Also the basic worldview is a very important point – what is the basic element in one's worldview? This can be the omnipotent One God, the aspired omnipotence of the magician, the life struggle of everyone against everyone, a benevolent Great Mother, the eternal change of all things, predestination, free will, the whole earth with all beings on it as a total living being … There are many possibilities – and out of all these views, on some occasions very different rituals are designed.

II 5. The Source of Power

The ritual is first of all only a form consisting of actions, gestures, words, etc. – a machine that still has to be connected to the current in order to run. Several "connections" come into question for this "current":

- the One God
- a deity
- the collective subconsciousness
- one's own soul
- a spirit

- one's own power animal
- the life force in general
- one's own Kundalini
- one's own will

These "power connections" look very different at first, but the variety is not quite as great as it seems to be:

- The life force is closely connected with consciousness – consequently, spirits are, so to speak, a part of the life force with a more or less conscious momentum of its own.

- The Kundalini is a section of the "life force circuit" in one's own life force body.

- The collective subconscious has telepathy and telekinesis as its "organs" of perception and action and is identical with the life force in all things.

- The archetypes in the collective subconscious consist of the images of all present and past images in the individual subconscious of the people.

- The archetypes in the collective subconscious are identical with the deities in the myths.

- One's own power animal, one's own power plant and one's own power stone are parts of the general life force or the spirits in the world, to which one has a special connection.

- The One God can be understood as the totality of consciousness in all things.

- A soul can be considered as a part of God.

All these sources of power are in the realm of consciousness. They differ mainly in the size of their part in the whole consciousness – one's own kundalini is only a very small part, while God encompasses everything.

This does not mean that God as a source of power is necessarily more effective than the Kundalini, because in the end the effectiveness of a ritual depends only on the fact that enough "current" for the "ritual machine" flows through the "connecting cable", which one has produced by a God invocation or the like.

It is also more than questionable whether one can simply transfer to the area of consciousness and life force the habits of thinking which are formed by the perception of the outer, material world. The existence of telepathy and telekinesis clearly shows

13

that things are not so clearly separated in the area of consciousness as in the area of matter.

So, in the end, one can only say that a source of power is needed for the ritual and that this source of power must correspond to the magician's world view and style.

II 6. The Participants

A ritual performed by a single person is easier to design, if only because the person may then compose and perform the ritual in his own style.

If the ritual is performed by two people, by a group, or by a large community, the style must fit everyone, improvisations are more difficult to perform, the movements, gestures, words, and imaginations of all participants must be coordinated, and so on.

On the other hand, an invocation to the gods, for example, can be extremely powerful when performed by a group that has been using this ritual regularly for a number of years.

The construction of an effective ritual, which can be easily grasped by all participants in its structure and which is also magically effective, is of course more demanding than a simple ritual performed by only one person.

There are, of course, many intermediate phenomena, such as rituals that have a clear leader and in which the other participants are only imagination helpers, who sing along with songs, who can only say something at certain points, etc.

II 7. The Layers

A ritual has more than one layer. At least seven different layers can be distinguished:

    - the goal of the ritual
    - the central element of the ritual
    - possibly a superordinate symbol, which is the basis of the ritual structure
(element circle, cabbalistic tree of life, I Ching, etc.)
    - the action, the gestures, the words, the temple, etc.
    - the symbolism of the actions, gestures, etc.
    - the different functions of the active participants
    - the (possibly different) deities invoked by the participants

Not every ritual has to be complex – this does not make it better or more effective. But a well-designed complex ritual can be very powerful.

The main thing is to be aware of these levels when designing and creating a ritual – simply because these levels exist. You can design a ritual very simply and it can be very effective – because you have paid attention to all the points that are relevant to the construction of a ritual. The ritual should be a good "machine" so that the "current" summoned in the ritual can start the "machine" well and the "current" is used effectively.

II 8. The Symbols

Symbols are used in almost every ritual. They are the pictorial expression of an often quite complex idea that evokes a large amount of associations in the observer. Symbols used in rituals can be used to represent transformation processes and many other dynamics in a simple way.

A very simple ritual is, for example, the consecration of a golden ring with a ruby, which one has forged to strengthen the power of Mars in oneself. You can put the ring in a ritual in front of a statue of the Greek god of war Ares, call Ares, ask him for the consecration of the ring and then wear this ring.

In a witch coven there are rituals in which a man holds his staff in the chalice of a woman. This symbolic sexual union is unmistakable to all participants.

It is useful, when using symbols, to consider what those symbols represent – the traditional meaning of a symbol will prevail over the meaning ascribed to it by its user. Some symbols, such as the snake, also have a long history, going back to the late Paleolithic – they therefore have layers of different ages in their symbolism, which it makes sense to consider.

However, it is generally better to just get started than to study for decades to be sure – the best foundation for magic is still your own experience. And failures are a solid basis for expertise.

II 9.   The Complexity

The complexity of a ritual can be markedly different:

- One can simply call the four elements in the four cardinal directions standardly with the Lesser Pentagram Ritual.

- One can also use the Great Pentagram Ritual and invoke all the archangels, angels, spirits, angelic hierarchies, etc., using the Enochia language, imagining the Tattwa symbols, invoking the four signs of the zodiac – Leo, Libra, Scorpio and Taurus, etc.

- One can also simply stand in the middle, turn in the four directions of the sky and nod one time with the head …

Complexity is neither a guarantor of effectiveness nor an obstacle to it. The selected degree of complexity depends on what one wants to achieve with the ritual.

For example, a long and detailed ritual can have the effect of virtually putting one into a ritual trance.

One can also perform a complex ritual in order to summarize the various aspects one has found on a subject in one "ritual picture". In this way, one consciously cleans up the area of images and symbols, integrates them all, and creates the basis for later, simpler rituals.

Some rituals, such as initiations, also have many aspects by nature, and it makes sense to depict them as well. The Mysteries of Eleusis, for example, extended over ten days. Also an American Indian vision quest usually lasts three days – although it is very simple in its structure and consists mainly of "waiting in silence".

Possibly the basis of the planned ritual is also a mythe, which is represented in the ritual. If there are five gods involved, the ritual can become quite complex already because of these five roles/invocations and the actions between these gods.

The complexity of the ritual depends primarily on the goal, the motivation, the number of participants, and the general theme of the ritual.

II 10.   The Arc of Suspense

A good ritual has a good arc of suspense. The parts follow one another logically and are so clearly designed that each participant can understand what is happening and why – although surprising twists and turns can also be beneficial. But they must be firmly anchored in the logic of the ritual.

One can simply follow the structure of the classical drama:

> Act 1: the characters are introduced
> Act 2: the conflict between the characters becomes clear
> Act 3: the conflict between the characters increases
> Act 4: the tension is maintained
> Act 5: the tension is resolved

Of course, a ritual cannot be conceived like a drama, because a ritual is not a play that is supposed to evoke feelings in the viewer, but a ritual is supposed to have a magical effect. But one can study a successful arc of suspension in good dramas – and rituals should have their own kind of an arc of suspension.

The following elements, among others, may belong to the arc of suspense of a ritual:

- the opening of the ritual place: the drawing of a protective circle, the consecration of the temple, the invocation of protective deities, the Lesser Pentagram Ritual, the lighting of the sweat lodge fire, etc.

- the introduction of the participants: this is important only in larger rituals

- the opening of the arc of suspense: a declaration of intention, the reference to a deity or a mythe or a role model, etc.

- the connection with the life force: invocations of a deity or deities by several people, the invitation of certain spirits to the ritual, a dream journey, a mantra meditation, etc.

- the main action: the consecration, the initiation, the transformation, the expansion, the blessing, etc.

- the placement of the main action: description of the possible further development, tracing in silence the effect of the main part, etc.

- farewell: thanking the gods and spirits, final prayers, etc.

- closing the ritual place: simple gesture, farewell to the gods and spirits, Lesser Pentagram Ritual, letting the sweat lodge fire burn out, etc.

This structure may, of course, be varied depending on the theme. For example, a ritual may have three main parts, such as the calling of the aspired ideal, the calling of the feared shadow, and the uniting and dissolving of the two so that the original, whole form can reappear.

It is only important that the structure of the ritual be coherent – its parts should fit together like the parts of a machine, or even better, like the organs of a body, and thus as a whole be able to produce the desired effect in an effective manner. The ritual should therefore be a clear, striking and memorable picture of the goal and the way to it.

Part of a good arc of suspense of a ritual is that the individual parts are of a measured length – that the opening, for example, does not take up half of the ritual.

It can be a good help in designing rituals if you have written stories, fairy tales, plays, or at least a few poems. This gives a feeling for a good measure and a good arc of suspense.

II 11. Old or New?

You can use an old, traditional ritual for a specific purpose. If you know one and the style of the ritual suits you, there is nothing to stop you from using it – especially since rituals that have been used many times develop a momentum of their own. One enters, so to speak, into resonance with all previous performances of this ritual. This can give you an extra boost.

If you don't know a ritual on the desired topic or the known rituals on the topic don't fit your own style and worldview, you should design a new ritual. It is possible to use elements of older rituals. When designing new rituals, most magicians treat tradition like a LEGO box: They build something new from the old elements.

You can also use traditional rituals and add your own texts to them. One can also strengthen certain traditional parts of a ritual, such as the Pentagram Ritual, with additions, if one feels that the ritual as a whole needs a firmer framework, a more secure vessel.

It is also advisable to participate once in different rituals and look at their structure, their dynamics, their intensity and, if possible, their effectiveness. In this way one can learn a lot about rituals – and about different styles.

The more different the rituals one participates in or at least studies, the more one can learn: a Christian monk's consecration, a sweat lodge ceremony, a Golden Dawn Initiation, a dervish dance, an ancestor dance of the Ewe in West Africa, an Indian soma ceremony, an American Indian sun dance, the Tapati Rapa Nui on Easter Island, the ancient Egyptian burial ritual, and so on.

II 12. The Conclusiveness

The conclusiveness of a ritual depends on many things: on the worldview under-lying the ritual, on the straightforwardness of the striving for the desired goal, on the inner logic of the chosen method, on the relationship of the parts of the ritual to each other, on the intensity of the connection to the life force, on the uniformity of the style, etc.

One element that can significantly promote the conclusiveness of a ritual is a cohe-rent ideological background to which the entire ritual is oriented. For example, the very complex initiation rituals of the Golden Dawn have been built in their basic structure on the Kabbalistic Tree of Life. As a result, they have a great clarity in their overall flow that holds together and effectively focuses the diversity of these rituals.

II 13. That "Certain Something"

The conclusiveness of a ritual can be recognized immediately, but it cannot be constructed or exhaustively described – just as a really good piece of music cannot be constructed and formally described. A good ritual, like a good piece of music, has something else that might best be called "inspiration" – it is something that comes from the depths, from one's heart chakra or from a deity. By this additional element the ritual or the piece of music gets that "certain something", a glow, a radiance … and its persuasive power …

Of course, there are also handicraft-good and simple rituals that serve their purpose, but if you have experienced, for example, once a sweat lodge ceremony, after which one of the participants, who had been a chain smoker, spontaneously and permanently gave up smoking, because in the sweat lodge she found again what she was actually looking for, then you know what this "certain something" is.

As preparation for the design of a ritual, one can also undertake dream journeys on the subject of the ritual or fast for a week to give emphasis to one's own search. In this way, one often comes to experiences or contacts with deities and spirits that com-pletely change one's view of the planned ritual.

II 14.   The Finishing Touch

After the goal has become clear and unambiguous, the ritual has been designed, all texts have been written, and any overemphasis on a part of the ritual has been corrected, the last thing to do is to "fine-tune" the ritual: one checks once again the images, the style, the meter, the symbols used, the planned design of the ritual location, etc.

III   Ritual Elements

A ritual can contain many different elements. There will hardly be a ritual that contains all of these elements – but after all this isn't necessary for a good ritual. All these elements are just tools to make the ritual as effective as possible – and you don't need all tools at once.

When choosing these elements, it is important to always keep the goal of the ritual in mind and to subordinate everything to this goal – otherwise the ritual will not be able to be coherent and unified.

The number of elements used also depends, among other things, on whether it is a one-magician ritual or a group ritual. In a group ritual, a greater number of tools are usually beneficial, as they coordinate the concentration and imagination of the participants. With quite experienced participants, who already know the ritual well, one can get by with fewer aids.

Of course, beginners should not be confused by too many tools.

III 1.   The Place

Mostly the place results from the planned ritual: the Mysteries of Eleusis took place in the Temple of Eleusis, the burial in the cemetery, the meeting of the Witch-Coven in the clearing in the forest, the meeting of the Freemasons in the Lodge-Temple etc..

However, sometimes you have several places to choose from – especially if you are performing a ritual alone or just in pairs. There is no "one right place" – one should simply feel out what suits the intended ritual best: the temple (if available), the forest clearing or one's own living room. Sometimes a ritual is needed immediately and one performs it imaginatively while sitting in a train compartment or at the wheel of one's broken down car on the highway.

A ritual may well be enhanced by performing it in a particular "place of power", but rituals are not generally dependent on the choice of a particular place – nevertheless, there are places that one will generally prefer for certain rituals. Thus, a mountaintop or the seashore is appropriate for a wind invocation, a temple for an initiation ritual, a cave for an otherworld journey, a temple or church for a consecration, etc.

III 2.   The Time

Sometimes the timing is largely self-evident, as in the case of baptisms, weddings, funerals, harvest rituals, and the like.

In general, one can say that full moon days or the two days before full moon are conducive for all rituals where something is to be changed or transformed – that is, for almost all rituals. Sweat lodge ceremonies also usually take place on a full moon or just before.

Sometimes the time also results from the biography: a Saturn ritual at the age of 28, when Saturn is again in the same position as it is in the birth chart of the person concerned; an initiation ritual when the person concerned has completed all preparations; baptism, confirmation, wedding, funeral; immediate help in an acute psychic crisis or psychosis; etc.

III 3.   The Circle of Protection

The circle of protection originates from the evocations, i.e. the calling of spirits and demons in the Middle Ages. The magician wanted to protect himself by such a circle from the spirits he summoned.

Nowadays, the protective circle is often used to create a "neutral place for a magic experiment" – it's like cleaning the vessels before doing a chemical experiment. The erection and dissolution of the protective circle then also marks the beginning and the end of a ritual.

There are also rituals where no protective circle is used – such as many rituals in witch covens. If one feels as part of nature and safe in nature, no demarcation towards nature is necessary …

Sometimes there is also a "permanent protection" in a place like the walls of a church or temple. The sweat lodge as a symbol of the belly of the pregnant Mother Earth is also such a permanent protection.

Whether one uses a protective circle in a ritual or not, therefore, depends very much on the worldview of the person concerned and, moreover, also on the planned ritual.

The protective circle is not an absolute necessity.

III 4. Deities and Spirits

Invoking deities or spirits is a central element in most rituals – from the Eucharist (Lord's Supper) to witchcraft rituals to spiritist sessions. In those rituals where gods or spirits are invoked, they are almost always the power source of the ritual.

Sometimes the gods are also models in an initiation, as in the monk's consecration Christ, or as in the initiation rituals of the Rosicrucians and the Golden Dawn Christian Rosenkreuz, who is ultimately identical with Christ. In the consecration of nuns, Christ is the spouse of the nun who marries him at her consecration. In the Osiris Mysteries, Osiris is the model for the people.

The spirits of the ancestors are often called to receive advice and help – as in the Germanic Utiseta, in the spiritualistic session and in the systemic family constellations.

III 5. Statues

When statues of deities are used in a ritual, these statues are a temporary body of the deity in question, which is called into that statue so that one has a "gateway" to the deity. Of course, it makes a big difference if you have a 5cm tall Osiris statue standing in front of you in your living room or a 2m tall Shiva statue in a temple. One can say quite flatly "the bigger the statue, the more dominant it is in the ritual".

A statue of a god consecrated with expertise in an ancient temple is something you don't have to explain further when you see it. For example, when you see the life-size statue of the lion goddess Sakhmet at Karnak in Egypt in the temple on the northern edge of the complex, your hair may stand on end. Such a statue has become much more than a ritual prop – the goddess lives in this statue.

Normally, however, one will not have such a statue available in one's rituals – nor will one have a temple nearby that has such a statue.

Similar powerful statues can be found in other places such as the statues of Christ, the apostles and the saints around St. Peter's Square in Rome.

III 6. Symbols

Symbols can be used to represent qualities in a ritual – by putting them in a certain place, by doing something with them, by consecrating them or changing them.

The deities are the fixed points, sources and models in a ritual – the symbols are the words one exchanges with them.

III 7. Objects

Often there are other objects used in the ritual that are not primary symbols such as candles, altar cloths, a chalice for the ritual drink, pillars to the left and right of the entrance to a special area, etc.

A very special object is the wand. Originally it was the symbol of the World Tree. As such, it was the symbol of seers and seeresses – they traveled inwardly up the World Tree to the gods and ancestors in the sky, from whom they learned what was happening far away or what would happen in the future. Over time, the symbol of magical power has become a source of magical power.

However, it is quite easily possible to do magic without a magic wand.

III 8. Mandalas

Mandalas are magical-spiritual maps. Some rituals are based on such maps – for example, the Golden Dawn initiation rituals on the Kabbalistic Tree of Life.

A mandala is a concentric inner map. A typical division of a mandala consists of five areas and four directions:

- outermost ring: body, outer world
- second outermost ring: life force, psyche
- second innermost ring: soul
- innermost ring: deities
- central circle: God

- east quarter of the rings: air
- south quarter of the rings: fire
- west quarter of the rings: Water
- north quarter of the rings: Earth

Such a mandala can be used to structure the way from the outer world to the inner world, from multiplicity to unity, and to recognize, experience and go this way step by step.

A mandala is usually associated with a variety of meditations and rituals. A mandala is, so to speak, a mega-structure in which a single ritual can be found.

Such mandalas are used on the one hand as a picture and on the other hand also as a structure on the ground in which the ritual participants move.

In terms of its function, a mandala corresponds to such graphic representations of inner connections as the circle of the four elements, the diagram of the Chinese Ba Gua, the Kabbalistic Tree of Life and so on.

III 9.   Clothing

In some rituals, special clothing is worn, depending on the particular culture or order – such as the liturgical vestments in the Christian church or the black robes in most Saturnian orders.

In sweat lodges, in some witchcraft circles, and in some Indian yogi grups ("digambara sadhus"), the special garb consists of nudity.

Wearing a special garment while performing rituals has a strong effect on most people – one enters a "ritual state".

III 10.   Talismans

A talisman is a consecrated object – it can be any object and the way of consecration can be extremely varied. As a rule, the shape of the object consecrated to a talisman fits the type of consecration – a crucifix for Christ, an ankh for Isis, a square piece of pewter for Jupiter, a sword for the martial power of Ares, etc.

A talisman has a specific function and task, which can vary greatly depending on the type of consecration. A talisman is, so to speak, a container for a spell – the effect of which starts in a ritual by using the talisman in the ritual.

The largest possible talisman according to this definition is a consecrated statue of a god in which the deity in question is present – or an entire temple with several consecrated statues of gods.

III 11.   Texts

The texts in a ritual have the function, on the one hand, of giving form to the will and, on the other hand, of coordinating the actions of the people involved in the ritual.

Most conspicuous in a ritual are the incantations, often written in ancient languages, and the invocations of the deities. In many cases these invocations also have lyrical qualities and some of them are real works of art. The poetic level of these invocations is not essential for the functioning of the invocations, but it facilitates the concentration and sometimes also the imagination.

Most of the texts are spoken by an individual, but there are also jointly spoken verses, jointly chanted names of God, and the like, as well as fixed verses that are alternately spoken by several people or groups, which sometimes occur in the same form in many different rituals.

The texts of a ritual are often perceived as the central element in a ritual. It is therefore worthwhile to put a little effort into the texts.

III 12.   Chants

More or less the same applies to the chants as to the texts. Some chants are sung by only one individual, others by all – and there are also refrains sung together and other forms of alternate chanting.

The chants, especially the mantras (short verses) and the chants (short stanzas) that are repeated for a long time, have a special effect that goes beyond the spoken texts: They stimulate an inner vibration.

This is meant quite literally: If one has chanted a Shiva chant for half an hour together with two dozen other people in front of a Shiva statue in a temple, one can come into an altered state of consciousness that stabilizes oneself. One is, so to speak, "filled with Shiva" and is "carried" by him.

Rituals in which chants play a major role usually have little other text and action. An exception to this are the sweat lodge rituals, in which both the texts and the chants play an important role.

III 13. Dances

Ritual dances are found mainly among the so-called primitive peoples and in magical-mythological religions. Among primitive peoples (especially in Africa) there are dances for almost all occasions – the whole body calls the life force, the ancestors and the gods: "Sweat your prayers!" In the magical-mythological worldviews (whose root is in the Neolithic period), the temple dance is a formative element.

One can divide the ritual dances into several groups:

- the individual dance of specialists

- the group dance of specialists, who all perform the same movements

- the group dance of specialists, in which all have a special role (e.g. in the myth performance)

- the group dance of all, in which all do the same (simple) movements for a long time (trance dance)

- the group dance of all, who follow with their movements a leader, who changes the sequence of movements from time to time

- the group dance of all, in which all standing in a circle make the same simple movements, but one after the other individuals improvise other movements for a short time in the middle of the circle

The dance creates a vibration even more than the song. Singing and even more so dancing has the advantage that the action is not so strongly controlled by the head. This allows dance to develop an archaic power that is not so easily achieved by other methods.

III 14. Planned Improvisation

In some rituals there is room for "planned improvisation." This is the case, for example, with the circle dances, in which everyone makes the same movements in the circle, and a single person or, on sometimes also several people dance in the circle, expressing what is inside them by dance movements. Another example is the "round" in the sweat lodge, where one by one all who wish can say something to the spirits who have been invited into the sweat lodge. This round can be a very intense part of the ritual – simply because everyone can get very personal here.

However, this "planned improvisation" is a rather rare element in rituals.

III 15. The Distribution of Tasks

In more complex rituals in which several people participate, there is often a division of tasks. Typical tasks in rituals are:

- the ritual leader
- the high priestess
- the guardian
- the fire keeper (in sweat lodges)
- the soul guide (in initiation rituals and in mysteries)
- the initiate
- the embodiments of a deity in a mythe

IV   The Effectiveness of Rituals

Rituals should be effective. However, there is no patent remedy for this, which everyone can apply always and on all occasions.

A clear goal, a thoroughly examined motivation, the choice of a suitable central element, a lyrical ritual text, a successful arc of suspense, and ideally a little inspiration are the basis for an effective ritual.

Of course, there are also effective rituals to which this description only partially fits, such as sigil magic, which, however, also only to a very small extent still belongs to ritual magic.

And ultimately, ritual magic is also a craft that cannot be learned from one moment to the next – and as with any craft, the same applies here: "Practice makes perfect."

V The Benefits of Rituals

The primary benefit of rituals is, of course, magical success. However, rituals also have some secondary benefits.

- The most obvious is the need to think deeply about the issue where one wants to change something with the help of a ritual. This may lead to new insights that help to formulate the goal more precisely and achieve it more easily. During this process, one can possibly also resolve one or the other inner contradiction.

- Through the intensive study of the topic, one will probably also gain a better overview of the history and the inner structure of this topic – both with regard to one's own biography and with regard to the general history of this topic.

- Looking more closely at a theme and arranging its elements and dynamics in a ritual also leads to a greater awareness and coalescence of the different aspects of the theme in question. This also allows a clearer orientation to-wards the goal and a clearer recognition of the way to get there.

- Last but not least, a ritual is also a good aid to concentration and imagina-tion.

VI   The Development of Ritual Practice

The use of rituals shows a clear developmental arc in practice, which is quite similar for most magicians and witches.

In this development, ten phases can be distinguished, which follow one another in approximately the order shown below. The phases shown overlap, of course, and may also occur in slightly different sequence, but the basic development is very common.

1. first contacts: One experiences a first ritual, participates in a second and third ritual, and finds that this is something one wants to know better. One feels that there is a potential in magic rituals that can significantly improve and enrich one's life. So one decides to learn ritual magic.

2. first structures: First of all, one will probably perform for oneself the rituals one first learned. In doing so, one will necessarily become more familiar with the structure of the rituals – the mandala that may underlie them (e.g., the four elements in the four cardinal directions and the light in the center) and their dynamics (e.g., the protection and strengthening provided by the Lesser Pentagram Ritual).

3. first practical applications: Presumably, these rituals will also have practical applications fairly soon – e.g., a money spell or the Pentagram Ritual for protection during a traffic check.

4. different traditions: Next, many aspiring magicians and witches will seek out other rituals, learn about invocations of deities, possibly participate in a demon summoning, experience a magical healing, participate in an African Sun Dance, etc. This broadens one's horizon considerably and also one's understanding of what magical rituals can be.

5. self-made rituals: It is quite conceivable that at this point at the latest one will also begin to design one's own rituals. At first, traditional ritual parts are combined with each other, then supplemented by self-made texts as well as by handed down texts, which one has rewritten for special applications, and finally rituals that one has designed completely new. From this point on, one develops a clearer and clearer sense for the structure, the dynamics and the effectivity of a ritual.

6. Complexity: The knowledge of different possibilities, styles and traditions leads in many cases to the design of more and more complex rituals, which contain all the elements that belong to a theme. As a result, these elements are compared with each other, their relationship to each other is examined, their most useful combination is analyzed, and so on. In this way, an increasing expertise of the whole field of ritual and its possibilities emerges. The rituals themselves thus become great mandalas, magnificent ceremonies and detailed magical operations.

7. One's own style: By studying different traditions and designing complex rituals, one's own likes and dislikes in ritual magic become clearer and clearer. One realizes how one prefers to do what, what kind of "magic lyricism" one likes best, what tools help one the most … one develops one's own style.

8. simplification of the rituals: The different elements that make up the complex rituals, after a while, become more and more comprehensible – in terms of their style and also in terms of their effectiveness and their relationship to each other. This makes it clearer what one wants to use in which ritual, which elements are ultimately the same, what has proven to be most effective, and so on. As a result, the rituals now become increasingly simpler again.
The apprentice gets to know everything, the journeyman can create a meaningful variety from it, and the master can create the simple and effective design.

9. shrinking of the rituals to simple gestures: With increasing practice in the simpler rituals, the concentration and the imagination become more and more independent of the rituals. Thus the rituals shrink more and more and become a few words and a few gestures – the ritual runs increasingly only in the consciousness.

10. shrinking of gestures to wishes: Finally, the few words and gestures turn into an inner "magic-attitude", which is completely without words and gestures – the magic becomes a relaxed and effortless wishing.

VII   Examples

The structure and dynamics of rituals can be most easily explained with a few examples. Naturally, it is most helpful to use examples from different traditions.

VII 1.   Horus Ritual

In ancient Egypt there was a small statue of Harpocrates ("Horus the child") in almost every village. He stood with his feet on a scorpion, a snake and a crocodile. Under the god and the three animals, a gutter with a spout ran along the base of the statue.

When someone had been bitten by a scorpion or a snake, one went to this statue, poured water over it and caught the water, which had flowed over the Horus child into the gutter and then at the spout out again. This water was then given to the bitten person to drink.

This simple healing ritual refers to the fact that Isis, the mother of Horus, in the myths once healed Horus from a scorpion bite.

By the bitten person drinking the water that had flowed over the statue of Horus, the healing of Horus by Isis was also transferred to him. This is a simple form of ritual based on analogy magic.

VII 2.   Skull bowl magic

In the Horus ritual, we also find the principle that contact connects – that is, it is a form of association magic. The contact consists of water flowing over the statue.

This form of simple ritual has also been adopted by Christians. Until the Middle Ages, it was common to obtain the blessing of a saint by going on pilgrimage to his skull relic and drinking water out of his skull. By doing so, one received the connection to that saint.

Since each saint was associated with certain miracles based on his biography, one could choose which saint was responsible for one's problem and then drink from his skull.

This tradition is also found among the Germanic tribes and in Tibet. It was probably once quite widespread.

VII 3.   War dance

In traditional African dances there is a special ritual leader: the master drummer. Many ritual dances consist of about a dozen different step sequences, all of the same length, e.g. eight 4/4 bars long. These sequences of steps each include certain turns, jumps, gestures, chants, alternate chants, shouts, and so on.

The master drummer has the task of seeing when the dancers have achieved what they were meant to do with the current dance sequence: gather the concentration, summon the ancestors, build a tension, and so on. When this has been achieved, the master drummer moves on to the next dance motif. For this, there is a simple system of communication between the master drummer, the other drummers and the dancers:

In most traditional dances, all the movement sequences in a dance have the same length, so they are all eight bars long, for example. Each of these movement sequences has a specific drum rhythm that is different from the rhythm of the other movement sequences. In particular, the part that the master drummer drums for each movement sequence is easily distinguishable.

When the master drummer sees that a movement sequence has been danced for a sufficient length of time, he changes at the beginning of a movement sequence to the drum rhythm of the part that is to follow next. The other drummers and the dancers hear the change in rhythm and know which movement sequence and drum rhythm should come next. The movement sequence, at the beginning of which the master drummer changed the rhythm, is initially still drummed by the other drummers in the previous way and danced by the dancers in the previous way. So for eight bars the master drummer already drums the beat of the next movement sequence. At the beginning of the next movement sequence, everyone changes to the new movement sequence that the master drummer announced by changing the rhythm at the beginning of the last movement sequence.

In this way, the master drummer has the opportunity to direct the life force – for example, when he sees that the dancers in a war dance have danced the movement sequence that serves to center in themselves long enough that most of the dancers are well centered and grounded, he can move on to the movement sequence that represents the attack.

The first year I studied African dance with Papafiu, we practiced a war dance. It was quite exhausting – jumps, circles around oneself, complex arm movements, striking with a wooden sword, alternating shouts between Papafiu and us, invocations of Chief Odessu, who once after a victory put the power of that victory into this dance ... and then also being careful not to step on anyone else's feet or accidentally hit them with the wooden sword ...

But why ever did the Ewe, to whom the Kalifis and Papafiu belong, do such a war dance before their wars? After that they were completely exhausted! And then the others could come and collect the warriors completely exhausted by the dance – if the others were sensible enough not to dance ...

Strangely enough, also the Greeks and the Indians and still other peoples knew war dances – actually it could not be that parallel with different peoples the same nonsensical behavior has developed or that an ancient nonsensical behavior has kept so long that one can find it even in historical time with different peoples ...

The answer to this question came unexpectedly from the tax office Bonn-Außenstadt, in whose archive and form store I worked at that time. The head of the tax office had once again issued a decree which I found simply inhumane and which could only be good for further consolidating the head's authority and stoking his subordinates' fear of him (he apologized to the department heads for his behavior after his retirement).

In the evening I went from the tax office to the African dance and was still quite angry about the provost – which is not usually my style at all. As we prepared for the dance, I stood there thinking about the provost and clenched my fists, thinking inwardly "So, Mr. Provost! You won't break me! Now let's see who is the stronger of the two of us!"

The effect of this decision on the war dance was amazing. Suddenly I didn't have to pay attention to my posture, my gestures, my facial expressions, the volume of my voice when calling Chief Odessu and similar things – all these things came as if by themselves from my decision to show my teeth to the headman of the tax office. There was tension in my movements, my stomping was warlike, I really struck with my sword, my voice could not be ignored ... and I did not feel any effort, but instead got more and more power – Odessu sent me the power of his dance.

When the dance was over, I didn't want to stop at all and continued dancing alone for a short while. I think the headman would have backed away from my mere glance after this dance.

I understood a lot during this dance: If you do something you don't want, you lose power – if you do something you want, you gain power. Therefore, you should do only those things that you want to do from your heart – and you should not refrain from doing things that you want to do from your heart. Then you really live and be what you are and do what you want.

This war dance has been a perfect ritual all along – it has even contained that "certain something": The power of the former victory that had been banished into this ritual by the Chief Odessu.

However, what had been missing for the functioning of the ritual at first was my motivation to perform exactly this ritual – I got this motivation only through the quarrel with the head of the tax office. There my African dance teacher Papafiu and the head of the tax office "cooperated" in a perfect way to make clear to me the meaningful attitude towards life and the essence of rituals ...

The movement sequences in this rather long war dance of the Ewe chief Odessu have approximately the following meaning:

- The master drummer summons all the dancers.

- The dancers align themselves with the master drummer.

- Calling the earth by stomping; grounding oneself.

- Making space: wide steps; the men wield swords, the women wands with horse tails.

- Calling and showing power: leaps.

- Alternating chant with the master drummer: declaration of war.

- Invocation of the Ewe chief Odessu, who once, after winning a battle, put the power of that victory into this dance: calling him aloud with all one's voice-power.

- The dancers stand still and look at the master drummer, who calls out to the dancers several times, to which they always respond with the same phrase: Combat readiness.

- Departure for the fight.

- The fight itself.

- Victory.

- Return.

VII 4.   Sweat lodges

The sweat lodge is the oldest known ritual. It originated about 600,000 years ago, when the people of that time in northern Eurasia had to protect themselves against the cold of the ice age by building heated huts.

A sweat lodge is a hemisphere made of branches and skins or blankets, where people sit naked around the hole in the middle of the floor of the lodge, where there are glowing stones, and call the ancestors and animal spirits by chanting. Today's saunas and spas have been derived from the sweat lodge, losing all magical-spiritual aspects.

In the most widespread sweat lodge tradition, the seven directions have the meanings listed below:

- East:	Eagle	= foresight, clarity
- West:	Snake	= detail, life force, kundalini
- North:	Bear	= independence
- South:	Buffalo woman	= community, security
- Top:	Grandfather Sky	= responsibility
- Bottom:	Grandmother Earth	= trust
- Center:	Wakan tanka	= the Great Mystery

In a sweat lodge ceremony there are several „special persons":

- the "water man", who leads the ceremony and who pours the water on the red-hot stones in the sweat lodge, calls the spirits, starts the songs etc. (the shaman-priest)

- the "fire man", who lights of the fire, in which stones are placed, and carries the red-hot stones into the sewat lodge

- several persons, who build the hut (the water-man and others)

- cleaning the hut and the participants with sage smoke (by the water man)

Today's sweat lodge ceremonies have approximately (without the many details) the following sequence of events:

- entering the lodge

1st round
- the "fire man" carries glowing stones into the hole in the middle of the hut
- the "water man" pours water over the glowing stones
- chant – invocation of the spirits – chant

2nd round
- the "fire man" fetches more glowing stones
- the "water-man" pours water over the glowing stones
- chanting – common meditation or similar – chanting

3rd round
- the "fire man" fetches more glowing stones
- the "water-man" pours water over the glowing stones
- chanting – individual conversation with the spirits (requests, thanks etc.) – chanting

4th round
- the "fire man" fetches more glowing stones
- the "water man" pours water over the glowing stones
- singing – thanks to the spirits – singing

- leaving the lodge

As a central theme that runs through the entire ceremony, the water man may choose the most diverse things. These include, for example, healings, petitions for peace in the world, the complementary opposition of the instinctiveness of the snake and the clarity of the eagle, the complementary opposition between the independence of the bear and the sense of community of the buffalo woman, the complementary opposition between the responsibility of the grandfather and the trust of the grandmother, the rising of the Kundalini, etc. There are almost unlimited possibilities.

There are also many different individual elements that can be used in the sweat lodge: For example, the water man may suggest to the people in the sweat lodge to travel down into the earth in their imagination through the hole with the glowing stones and see what they find there. He can also ask them to ask the bear in the north to show them what is most important to them. He can also take the glowing stones as a symbol of the communal root chakra of the people in the sweat lodge, and the heat rising from the stones as the Kundalini rising.

However, the theme that is in the background of all variations of the ceremony is protection in the Mother Goddess – in the sweat lodge, the Buffalo Woman in the South and Grandmother Earth.

VII 5.   Kabbalistic Cross

The Kabbalistic cross has several functions: It is a sign of blessing, a sign of protection, and it can be used in rituals as a punctuation mark, so to speak, as a period, comma, and semicolon to delineate individual ritual parts from one another.

The kabbalistic cross refers to the sephiroth (areas) of the Kabbalistic Tree of Life.

The Kabbalistic Cross		
Words (Aramaic)	*Translation*	*Gesture*
Ateh	Yours is	the left hand comes down from above and touches the forehead with the fingertips
Malkuth	the kingdom	the left hand draws the line that began above the head, further down until the hand points to a point below the feet, marking the vertical bar
ve-Geburah	and the power	the fingertips of the left hand touch the right shoulder
ve-Gedulah	and the glory	the fingertips of the left hand go over to the left shoulder and touch it, thereby drawing the crossbeam of the cross
le-Olam, Amen.	forever, amen.	both hands are folded in front of the chest, symbolically connecting the two beams, imagining a red rose at the point of intersection

VII 6. Lesser Pentagram Ritual

This ritual creates a protective space on the one hand and charges this space with life force on the other hand. It can therefore be used in many ways in magic.

It is structured as follows:

- Kabbalistic cross:	centering
- Circle:	Protection
- Pentagrams:	Protection, invocation of the elements
- Archangel invocation:	invocation of the elements
- Kabbalistic Cross:	centering

The Ritual:

1. Kabbalistic Cross: *"Ateh Malkuth ve-Geburah ve-Gedulah le-Olam Amen."*

2. With the index and middle fingers of the right hand, indicate the drawing of the circle on the ground, imagining the circle – repeat twice; making the circle clearer each time.

3. Draw with the hand (gesture and imagination) the eastern pentagram (an up-right pentagram pointing upwards with one point and downwards with two points; one starts from the bottom left to the top center, further to the bottom right, to the left center, horizontally to the right center, to the bottom left). Hold your hand in the center of the imagined pentagram and chant, *"Yod-He-Vau-He"* (element of air);

4. In the same way, draw the southern pentagram and chant *"Adonai"* (element of fire).

5. In the same way, draw the western pentagram and chant *"Eheieh"* (element of water).

6. In the same way, draw the northern pentagram and chant *"Agla"* (element of earth).

7. Stand in the cross posture (arms stretched out to both sides) facing east and say and imagine:

"In front of me Raphael (yellow-violet archangel of the air, holding a sword, in the background clouds),

behind me Gabriel (blue-orange archangel of water, holding a chalice, in the background the sea),

to my right hand Michael (red-green archangel of fire, holding a staff, in the background flames),

to my left hand Auriel (lemonyellow-olivegreen-redbrown-black archangel of the earth, holding a coin or a round bread, in the background fields, pastures and forests),

I stand in the middle of the circle (strengthen the imagination of the circle), *around me are flaming pentagrams and above me radiates the six-pointed star* (hexagram = symbol of the seven planets with the sun in the center)."

8. Kabbalistic Cross: *"Ateh Malkuth ve-Geburah ve-Gedulah le-Olam Amen."*

VII 7. Extension of the Lesser Pentagram Ritual.

If one feels the need to protect the ritual site even more, the following four points can be added to the pentagram ritual:

1. Imagine the ritual place as an island and spray water (real water or only imagined water) at the edge of the circle as you walk along it in a clockwise direction, saying, *"So therefore, the priest who governeth the works of fire must sprinkle with the lustral water of the loud resounding sea."*

2. Imagine a blaze of light along the edge of the island, walking along the edge of the island with a burning stick of incense (symbol of fire), and say: *"And when, after all the phantoms are vanished, thou shalt see that holy and formless fire, that fire which darts and flashes through the hidden depths of the universe, hear thou the voice of fire!"*

3. Imagine a pillar of light (Middle Pillar) in the center of the island and say: *"Holy art Thou, Lord of the Universe! Holy art Thou, whom nature has not created! Holy art Thou, the One-All-Only!"*

4. Kabbalistic Cross: *"Ateh Malkuth ve-Geburah ve-Gedulah le-Olam Amen."*

The symbolism of this extension is the identification of the ritual place with the primordial island, which in many myths rose from the waters at the beginning of time. In the Bible, this has become the separation of water and earth by God.

The fire is the "ring of fire", thus the gate to the otherworld. It is also the fire in which the phoenix is reborn in the morning. With the phoenix the fire is the gate of the otherworld and at the same time the red sky in the morning. The phoenix and the fire bird corresponding to it in Slavic mythology is the soul bird of the sun, which is reborn in the morning in the fire of the morning red. The ring of fire is likewise the ritual fire of Agni, with which in former times in India each ritual was opened.

The texts of this extension come from the mystery cults. This extension, like the Lesser Pentagram Ritual itself, was also designed by the Golden Dawn.

In the original, it does not say "the One-All-Only" at the end, but "Lord of Light and Darkness". Since I do not really like this polar view (which is very formative in the Persian Zend-Avesta), I have replaced this term for "God" with another one that better describes my own view.

VII 8.   Greater Pentagram Ritual

This ritual is an extension of the Lesser Pentagram Ritual. The part that is expanded is the four pentagrams. In this ritual, the same pentagram is not drawn in each direction, but the special pentagrams that belong to each element. Before that, in each case, the pentagram of the quintessence ("spirit") is drawn, which is the center of the element mandala and the source of the four elements. Following these two pentagrams, which are drawn and imagined one after the other in the respective direction, one greets the respective element with a certain gesture.

This ritual is more complex, since in it different ways of drawing the pentagrams are used and since significantly more different invocation names are used. However, this ritual is much more powerful than the Lesser Pentagram Ritual. The Lesser Pentagram Ritual is primarily a protection ritual; the Greater Pentagram Ritual is primarily an invocation of the four elements.

Once you perform this ritual in the morning, at noon and in the evening for two weeks, you will be "charged" in such a way that it can have an effect similar to Kundalini Yoga: Everything hidden in the psyche is charged with life force in such a way that it moves and becomes visible, i.e., conscious.

1. Perform the Kabbalistic Cross.

2. Draw the circle.

3. East (air):

a) Spirit Pentagram:
   - Draw the Pentagram from bottom right to center left onwards. While doing so vibrate: *"Ex-ar-peh"*.
   - Draw a circle with four crossing lines (⊛) in the center of the pentagram; vibrate: *"Eheieh"*.

b) Invoking Pentagram of Air:
   - Draw the Pentagram von center right to center left onwards; vibrate: *"Oro Ibah Aozpi"*.
   - Draw the sign of Aquarius (♒) in the center of the pentagram; vibrate: *"Yod He Vau He"*.

c) Greeting of Air:
   - both arms sideways, lower arm upwards, hand upwards

4. South (fire):

a) Spirit Pentagram:
   - Draw the Pentagram from bottom right to center left onwards. While doing so vibrate: *"Bitom"*.
   - Draw a circle with four crossing lines (⊛) in the center of the pentagram; vibrate: *"Eheieh"*.

b) Invoking Pentagram of Fire:
   - Draw the Pentagram von center right to center left onwards; vibrate: *"Oip Teaa Pedoce"*.
   - Draw the sign of Leo (♌) in the center of the pentagram; vibrate: *"Elohim"*.

c) Greeting of Air:
   - both arms sideways, lower arm to the forehead, hands and thumps form a triangle (thumbs horizontal, fingers diagonal upwards to the center)

5. West (water):

a) Spirit Pentagram:
- Draw the Pentagram from bottom left to center right onwards. While doing so vibrate: *"Hcoma"*.
- Draw a circle with four crossing lines (⊕) in the center of the pentagram; vibrate: *"Agla"*.

b) Invoking Pentagram of Water:
- Draw the Pentagram from center left to center right onwards; vibrate: *"Empeh Arsel Gaiol"*.
- Draw the sign of Scorpio (♏) in the center of the pentagram; vibrate: *"Al"*.

c) Greeting of water:
- both arms sideways, lower arm to the breast, Hands and thumps form a triangle (thumbs horizontal, fingers diagonal downwards to the center)

6. North (earth):

a) Spirit Pentagram:
- Draw the Pentagram from bottom left to center right onwards. While doing so vibrate: *"Nanta"*.
- Draw a circle with four crossing lines (⊕) in the center of the pentagram; vibrate: *"Agla"*.

b) Invoking Pentagram of Earth:
- Draw the Pentagram von center right to center left onwards; vibrate: *"Emor Dial Hectega"*.
- Draw the sign of Taurus (♉) in the center of the pentagram; vibrate: *"Adonai"*.

c) Greeting of Air:
- right arm to the front diagonally upwards (45°); left arm to the back diagonally doenwards (45°)

7. Calling the four archangels as in the Lesser Pentagram Ritual.

8. Perform the Kabbalistic Cross.

VII 9. Planetary Hexagrams

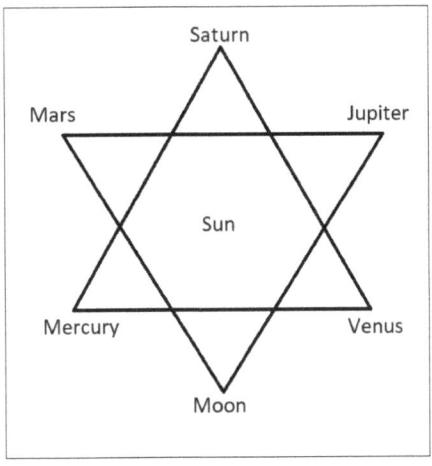

The pentagrams refer to the four elements and the quintessence, while the hexagrams refer to the seven classical planets.

The planets are assigned to the tips and the center of the hexagram – see the graphic on the left. Exactly the same arrangement of the planets can be found on the Kabbalistic Tree of Life.

The use of these hexagrams in the ritual is simple: with them the planetary qualities can be called.

To know the effect of the hexagrams one can use a simple ritual: The hexagram of the chosen planet is drawn one after the other in the east, south, west, north, bottom, top and then three times in the center, chanting the corresponding names.

When drawing the first of the two triangles that make up the hexagram, always start from the tip of the planet in question, that is, e.g. from the bottom in the case of the Moon. In the case of the Sun, which is in the center, the starting point does not matter – you may choose the tip you want.

When you draw the second hexagram, you start at the opposite point – e.g. for the moon at the top.

If you want to call the planetary force, draw the two triangles of the hexagram clockwise; if you want to banish it, counterclockwise.

Third, draw the planet symbol in the honeycomb area in the center of the hexagram.

While drawing these three lines (first triangle, second triangle, plantary symbol), the following names are chanted:

Moon:	1. Shaddai	2. el-Chai	3. Ararita
Mercury:	1. Elohim	2. Tzabaoth	3. Ararita
Venus:	1. Jehovah	2. Tzabaoth	3. Ararita
Sun:	1. Jehovah	2. Eloah va-Da'ath	3. Ararita
Mars:	1. Elohim	2. Gibor	3. Ararita
Jupiter:	1./2. El (this Name is rather short)		3. Ararita
Saturn:	1. Jehovah	2. Elohim	3. Ararita

These planetary hexagrams can be used in many different rituals to invoke the power and quality of a planet and to incorporate them into the ritual.

VII 10. Talisman Consecration

A talismanic consecration can be done in many different ways. The following is a simple, general method that can be used for just about any consecration:

1. Lesser Pentagram Ritual

2. invocation of the appropriate element
3. directing the power of the element into the talisman
4. pronouncing the purpose (task) of the talisman as a statement of the goal achieved, e.g. *"I am healthy."*

5. invocation of the appropriate planet
6. directing the power of the planet into the talisman
7. pronouncing the purpose (task) of the talisman as a statement

8. invocation of the appropriate deity
9. asking the deity to direct the power into the talisman
10. pronouncing the purpose (task) of the talisman as a statement

11. Lesser Pentagram Ritual

VII 11. Snake Rings

It is also possible to make much more individual consecrations. I used the following method when I was still a "sorcerer's apprentice". At that time I made once thirteen magic rings, i.e. I forged and consecrated them. I forged them to bury them at powerplaces and on crossings of leylines etc. to help the wood against the acid rain.

- Forging twelve rings with a tourmaline in the serpents head and a larger, central, thirtenth ring with a ruby on the serpents head.

- Writing an invocation to the power of serpents and dragons as a song with

46

meter, end rhyme, refrain, etc.

- Singing these invocations while forging the rings.

- Imagining the power of the serpents in the rings.

- Analogy of forging the rings to a pregnancy.

- All operations are performed on the full moons in the nine months of this "pregnancy".

- On each full moon the same is done for all the rings: drawing the parts that need to be sawn out on the silver; sawing out; welding the silver strands together to form a ring; filing, placing the setting for the gemstone on the head of the snakes; polishing the snakes, etc..

- Beginning of the forging work at Easter, so that the "birth" of the snakes could take place on the full moon near the night of Jul (21. 12.), which in the myths is the time of the rebirth of the sun.

These rings were very powerful. However, I had not thoroughly checked my motivation nor the symbolism beforehand, so in the end these rings only caused a big mess, when the quality of these rings bedcame obvious: might over others and over circumstanves, repressed sexuality, the rings of power in the stories of J.R.R. Tolkien and so on.

I had overlooked completetly the striking similarity of these rings and their production with the magic rings from the "Lord of the Rings" …

I could also have strengthened the effect of the rings by rubbing them with a homeopathic snake remedy in the potency C200 on every full moon – preferably a cobra remedy, since the cobra represented the Kundalini in India and in ancient Egypt. Perhaps it would have been even more effective to start with the highest potency and then move to a lower and lower potency.

But at that time I did not know much about homeopathy – which may have been a good thing, because otherwise the power of the rings might have become even greater and also the desaster at the end …

VII 12.   The Middle Pillar Exercise

This ritual connects with God and invokes a blessing from Him. It can be used in many ways as a part of more complex rituals – e.g. as centering, strengthening and protection. It also enhances the effect of many exercises such as kundalini awakening, letter exercises and the like. The effect of drugs is also increased by this exercise.

1. A few handbreadths above the head Kether is imagi-nated as a glistening white sphere and at the same time God's name of Kether is intoned, i.e. sung on a constant tone as full-sounding as possible and ideally with over-tones and the natural vibrato of the voice: *"Eheieh"*.

> "Kether" and the other following four Hebrew names of the Sephi-roth designate the five areas on the Middle Pillar of the Kabbalistic Tree of Life. The names that are chanted are the traditional names of God from the Old Testament that designate this area. However, these names from the original Hebrew of the Old Testament are often not literally translated into German in the Bible, but are simply translated as "God" or "Yahweh."
>
> This chanting has similarities with Gregorian chanting and with the Indian and Tibetan way of chanting mantras. This kind of intonation of "holy words" is found among almost all peoples – for example, the ancient Egyptian magicians praised their magic texts in the papyri as "spells that can be sung well" and in the Germanic myths and sagas it is mentioned again and again that things are consecrated, i.e. charged with magical power, by singing into them ("He sang runes into the sword."; "He sang runes into the stem of the dragon boat."). Of the Druids it is told, that, when doing magic, their voices sounded like the voice of a stag.
>
> However, simply chanting the names of the gods as sonorously as possible is quite sufficient for starters.

2. On the crown, that is, at the seat of the crown chakra, Da'ath is imagined as a sphere shining in the colors of the rainbow, intoning Da'ath's name of God: *"Yod-He-Vau-He Elohim."*

3. In the center of the chest, that is, at the seat of the heart chakra, Tiphareth is imagined as a sphere shining in golden colors, and the name of God of Tiphareth is intoned: *"Yod-He-Vau-He Eloha va-Daath"*.

4. Around the genitals, i.e. at the seat of the root chakra and thus of the kundalini snake, Yesod is imagined as a violet glowing sphere and the name of God in Yesod is intoned: *"Shaddai el-Chai"*.

5. Under the feet, i.e. in the earth, Malkuth is imagined as a brown sphere and the name of God's of Malkuth is intoned: *"Adonai ha-Aretz"*.

In the following table the areas, the Sephiroth, the colors, the places and the names of God are summarized:

The Middle Pillar				
Area	*Sephirah*	*Color*	*Place*	*Name of God*
unity (God)	Kether	white	Sky	*Eheieh*
boundless area	Da'ath	rainbow colors	Crown Chakra	*Yod-He-Vau-He Elohim*
demarcated area	Tiphareth	golden	Heart Chakra	*Yod-He-Vau-He Eloh va-Daath*
internal area	Yesod	violet	Root Chakra	*Schaddai el-Chai*
multiplicity (world)	Malkuth	brown	Earth	*Adonai ha-Aretz*

VII 13. Isis Invocation

One can build invocations in the same way as the talismanic consecration already described. An Isis invocation would then look like this:

1. Lesser Pentagram Ritual

2. invocation of the water
3. filling the room with the element of water
4. connecting with the water

5. invocation of the moon
6. filling the room with the quality of the moon
7. filling oneself "with moonlight"

8. calling of Isis
9. conversation with Isis
10. invocation of Isis

11. Lesser Pentagram Ritual

In this ritual one can use symbols such as the ankh ("life"), the posture of Isis (from her representations in Egypt), small dream journeys within the ritual, original invocations e.g. from the Isis temple in Philae, etc.

VII 14. The Integration of the Shadow

The shadow is that part of one's psyche that is present as a need and an ability, but that has never been developed or even has been repressed. It is the part of one's psyche that one fears and avoids – one's personal devil …

As a basis for the integration of this shadow, one can use various symbolisms. One of them is the concept of the Sephiroth and the Qlippoth in the Kabbalah. The Sephiroth represent the attributes of God, the Qlippoth their shadow sides or the deviations from them – one could also say that the Sephiroth are the anatomy of God and the Qlippoth the anatomy of the devil.

The interpretation of the Qlippoth depends very much on one's worldview. One way is to view them as a differentiated representation of the possible forms of the shadow.

The eleven sephiroth or qlippoth represent the entire world: the body, the psyche (subconscious, thinking, feeling), the soul, the deities and the One God. Therefore, the Qlippoth also include all possible deviations from the healed state or all conceivable types of shadow.

On this basis, a ritual for the integration of the shadow can be designed:

- Lesser Pentagram Ritual
- Asking one's own soul for help and guidance in the ritual.

- The invocation of the eleven Sephiroth – each receives a place in the temple in the arrangement of the Sephiroth on the Tree of Life.
- Invocation of the eleven Qlippoth – each receives a place in the temple in the arrangement of the Qlippoth on the Tree of Life.

- One by one, the paired Sephiroth and Qlippoth are brought together – symbolically by putting the symbols together or something similar.
- Contemplating the quality that shows itself during the meeting of the Sephiroth and the Qlippoth – possibly in a short dream journey each.

- Possibly resolutions to a new, more integrated way of life.
- Thanks to one's own soul.
- Lesser Pentagram Ritual

VII 15. Relationship Mandala

The Relationship Mandala is based on a simple inner dynamic that results from the structure of the psyche:

- In the beginning is the incarnating soul,
- then the psyche comes into being and
- finally, the essence of the psyche is enacted and experienced in the world through relationships with other people in "dramatic form".

The structure that emerges can be represented as a mandala:

- innermost circle: the soul and its intention for its current incarnation

- inner ring: the male reflection of the soul in the life force (inner whole man) and the female reflection of the soul in the life force (inner whole woman)

- outer ring: the two polarized images of man and woman, respectively, created by violent experiences
There are three possibilities of polarization:
- fullness   => lack   => addict + ascetic;
- power   => violence   => perpetrator + victim;
- self-love   => self-doubt   => star + fan

- the four triangles on the outside: the four roles created by this polarization.

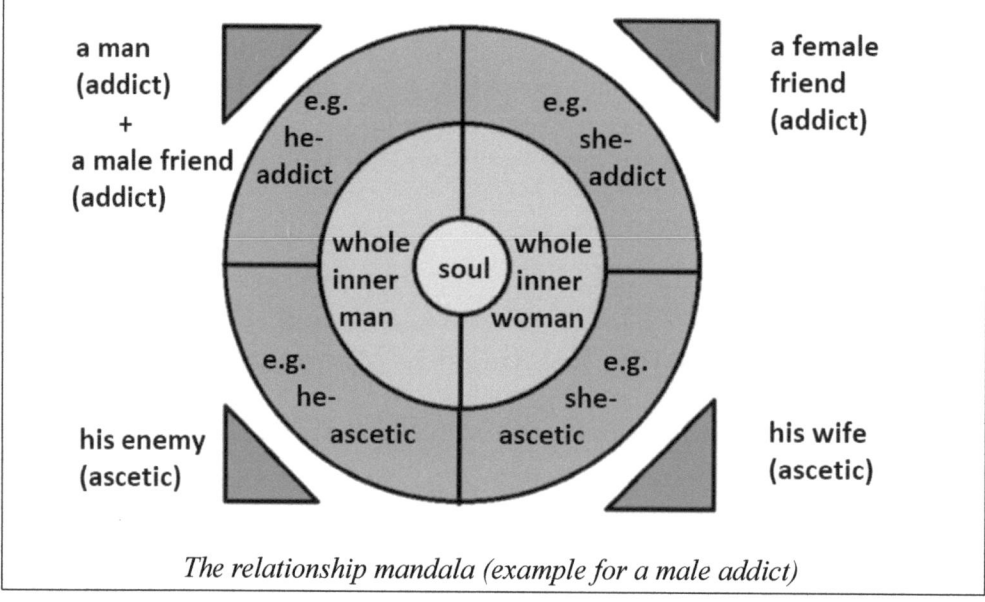

The relationship mandala (example for a male addict)

One of these four polarized images (triangles) is lived by oneself – in this example the male addict. The corresponding female image ("she-addict") would then be a girlfriend. The opposite of this, i.e. the ascetic and the ascetic woman, also have certain functions: The male ascetic the role of the enemy and the female ascetic the role of the relationship partner.

The healing of the self-image and relationships includes four steps, which also make up the sections of the corresponding ritual:

> 1. the recognition of the four roles in one's own life drama

> 2. the realization that other people play roles that one carries within oneself and that one makes available to them (the male addict carries within himself the image of the female addict, the male ascetic and the female ascetic, but lives himself only the image of the male addict – the other three images are taken over by other people)

> 3. the dissolution of the two polarities (two male extremes, two female extremes)

> 4. the union of the healed inner man with the healed inner woman

The alchemical symbolism can be used for this, because the production of the philosopher's stone is also based on the idea that in the beginning there was a right state, but then it was distorted by a polarization, which can be dissolved again by alchemy.

The complete ritual can be found in my book "Das Beziehungs-Mandala".

VII 16.   The Mysteries of Eleusis

This probably most famous of all rituals has a complex structure. Like all mysteries, it is a ritual otherworld journey that helps the participant make contact with his or her own soul: "Know Thyself."

Under the direction of the Archon Basileus ("High King" = high priest) of Athens, a pig was first sacrificed to Demeter or Persephone. Sometimes the participants themselves sacrificed a piglet to one of the two goddesses. Afterwards the priests purified themselves by bathing in the river Ilissos, and then purified all those participating in the mysteries.

> => The soul was conceived in the early religions as the child of the mother goddess.
> => The purification in the river has the same symbolism as the baptism: a journey to the water underworld to get in touch with the gods.

The mysteries lasted 10 days. Four groups of people participated in them, and men, women and also slaves were allowed:

1. the priests, priestesses and hierophants (high priests)

2. the men and women who participated in the ceremony for the first time – the condition for participation was:
        a) not to have committed murder,
        b) to be able to speak Greek fluently,
        c) the oath of secrecy.

3. persons who had already participated in the ceremony

4. persons who had been initiated into the secrets of Demeter and had learned the epopteia ("contemplation")

The visitors who accompanied the celebrations and especially the procession along the sacred road did not participate directly in the Mysteries.

The Mysteries were conducted by the Hierophant ("Revealer of the Sacred Mysteries"), who was the chief priest in the Temple of Demeter at Eleusis. He was considered the successor of the mythical founder of the Mysteries (Eumolpos or Triptolemos).

The actions at the Mysteries proceeded as follows:

previous day: The sacred objects of Demeter were brought to the temple of Eleusinion at the foot of the Acropolis.
      => Demeter, as the mother goddess, is also the mother of souls.

1st day: The official beginning was called "Agyrmos" (assembly). The Hierophant performed a sacrifice called "Hiereia Deuro" ("Bring the sacrifices").
      => The sacrifices will origonate from the funeral customs in which a herd animal was sacrificed to the dead traveling to the otherworld. The ones to be consecrated also symbolically traveled to the otherworld.

2nd day: The priests purified themselves in the sea in Athens.
      => This is probably again the water underworld symbolism.

3rd day: A pig was sacrificed to Demeter or Persephone. Afterwards one took part in the celebration of the healer Asklepios in Epidauros.
   => The pig has again the funeral and afterlife journey symbolism.

4th day: On this day the participants of the mysteries had to stay at home and were not allowed to leave the house. They probably made the later used ritual potion (Kyknos) on this day.

5th day: Starting from the Athenian cemetery Kerameikos outside the city walls, everyone went in procession along the 21 km long "Sacred Way" to Eleusis: in front the priests holding up the tablets of Dionysus, and behind them the participants of the Mysteries garlanded with myrtle branches. At certain sections of the road, called Bacchoi, the participants waved their Bacchoi staffs.
   => These sticks could have symbolized the world tree as the way to the otherworld. It could also have represented the penis of Bacchus – then it would be a reference to the re-procreation that preceded the re-birth.

At a fixed point the participants shouted obscene jokes because the maid Jambe had made the goddess Demeter smile with such a crude joke during her search for Persephone.
   => This scene, which is also found in other mysteries and even in myths in Japan, is an allusion to the re-procreation.

During the procession the participants called again and again with *"Iakche, o Iakche!"* to the god Dionysos.
   => Since Dionysus is a god who goes the way to the underworld, he was the model for those to be initiated.

When the procession arrived at the temple of Iakchos (Dionysus), the statue of the god was taken from it and then carried in the procession further on to Eleusis.
When the participants passed the last bridge on their way, they received a thread tied to their right hand and left foot by a priest.
   => This bridge symbolized probably the passage over the beyond river Styx.
   => The thread could then be an equivalent to the thread with whose help Perseus found his way out of the labyrinth of the Minotaur at Knossos, symbolizing the underworld.

On arrival at the temple, Demeter's search for Persephone was represented by the participants being led through the hall on wrong paths and finally arriving at the well (gate to the underworld) and visiting the cave of Plouton (Hades, the God of the dead) on the temple grounds (underworld gate).

6th day: On this day the participants in Eleusis fasted as Demeter had fasted during her search for Persephone. In the evening, at the end of the fast, everyone drank the kykeon, a drink made from barley and women's mint, which may have also contained extracts from the ergot (LSD source substance).
=> Fasting is a symbol of the stay in the underworld.

7th day: In the morning, everyone entered the Telesterion temple hall, which measured 52m·52m and whose roof was supported by 6 rows of 7 Ionic columns each. It had a pyramidal roof that could be opened at the top center as a smoke outlet. In this hall there was enough space for 7,000 people. Outside on the perimeter were benches for those who were only passively participating. In the center was the roofless anactoron ("palace") containing the sacred objects. In this sanctum, during the Mysteries that day, the sacred relics of Demeter were shown to those who were to be initiated.
The proceedings in the Anactoron began with the hierophant striking a gong symbolizing thunder and calling back the goddess Persephone from the underworld.
=> This corresponds to the Indo-European mythology of the thunder god, who was originally the weather god returning from the underworld in autumn. Since this symbolism ultimately goes back to the underworld journey of the vegetation god and the sun god, the thunder here corresponds to the returning Persephone. At this point there was also a loud call – presumably for Persephone.

In the Anaktoron now such a large fire was kindled that it shone up through the vent of the temple, so that one could see it even from outside the temple.
=> This corresponds to the fire in which Demeter would have given Triptolemos his immortality, if she had not been disturbed by his parents. The fire is like the torches of Persephone the gate to the underworld (the later hell was identified with this fire). This fire is found in the Druids and also in the later Christian Greek as the fire walk. It also corresponds to the Agni fire in India as well as the phoenix in Egypt and the fire bird of the Slavs.

The tension will have been greatest at this time. Aelius Aristides says of it, "Eleusis is at once the most terrible and the most luminous of all that is divine to men." Plutarch describes the Mysteries in much the same way: "Wandering around at first, wearying circumambulations, fearful happenings in the dark that find no goal; then immediately before the end all the awful, shuddering, trembling, sweating, and wondering."

Plutarch's description also describes in a figurative way very aptly the processes of healing a trauma – the Mysteries were also a method of fundamental healing of man …

When the hierophant finally opened the gate of the Anaktoron, he called out, *"The Lady* (Demeter) *has given birth to a holy child, Brimo* ("the strong one") *has given birth to Brimos* ("the strong one")*!"* At this the hierophant showed a sheaf of grain.

Belonging to this passage there is a fragment from a narrative about Heracles, in which, after not being admitted to the Mysteries of Eleusis, he says to the hierophant, "I have already been initiated elsewhere. Hierophant, close Eleusis – and Daduchos, put out the fire! I have already been initiated into more real mysteries! I have looked into the fire and I have seen Kore!" This refers to the fact that Heracles has been in the underworld when he took the hellhound Cerberus.

From this it follows incidentally that Dionysus and Heracles were both gods and demi-gods, respectively, who represented the successful journey to the otherworld and back again – Dionysus above all illustrating ecstasy and Heracles, by his 12 labors, above all illustrating the difficulties on the way (of the sun) through the underworld. The twelve works correspond to the twelve signs of the zodiac through which the sun passes each year.

> => The child (Brimos) that was born was Persephone, who is the re-born Demeter (Brimo) – in this myth the symbolism of the vegetation god and the weather god was transferred to the goddess herself. The underworld journey of a goddess exists outside the Indo-European mythologies only in the Sumerian goddess Inanna. Demeter and Persephone were regarded by the Greeks as the same goddess, once as a girl and once as a woman.

The symbolism of the journey to the underworld is also shown in the comment of Pindar around 450 B.C.: "Well is he provided, who under knowledge of Eleusinian wisdom climbs into the tomb. He knows the exit of material life and its God-given restart." This passage may be an indication that in the Eleusinian Mysteries, as by Pythagoras and Orpheus, reincarnation was taught.

In the Anaktoron there was a "Kalathos" (open basket), in which there was a "box" (crate), in which there was again the Holy of Holies.

> => There is the assumption that there were ears of corn or a golden snake, an egg or a phallus – but one does not know it, because the object or the objects remained just secret. The ears of corn, however, are unlikely, since the hierophant had already shown a handful of ears of corn to those present earlier in the ritual.

Upon returning from the Anaktoron (Holy of Holies) to the Telesterion (Great Hall), those to be initiated said, *"I fasted, I drank the Kykeon, I took it out of the box, and after I had it, I put it back into the Kalathos."*

The events and actions in the Anaktoron were the greatest mystery of the Mysteries. Their betrayal was punishable by death. These secret things were called apporheta ("unrepeatable things"). They consisted of three things:

> 1. dromena ("things that are done") – probably a ritual representation of Demeter's otherworld journey, through which the initiate also traveled to the otherworld;
> 2. deiknumena ("things that are shown") – sacred things that were shown by the hierophant;
> 3. legomena ("things that are said") – comments that were said by the hierophant about the things that were shown.

8th day: The priestesses announce in the morning in the Telesterion their visions from the last night, which was called the "Holy Night".

The Hierophant, together with the Daduchos (the second highest priest of Eleusis) sang the praises of Demeter and her daughter Persephone on this day. "Daduchos" ("torch-holder") was also the epithet of Artemis and Demeter when the latter searched for her daughter Persephone in the darkness (underworld) with torches.

In the evening and throughout the night, the festival of Pannychis was celebrated with dancing and merriment. At the dance, the newly consecrated men, like Dionysus, wore girls' dresses, which probably illustrated their identity with Persephone, i.e. their return from the underworld. The dance site was the Rharic Fields, which are said to have been the first place where crops were grown after Demeter showed Triptolemos how to cultivate them.

Towards morning a bull was sacrificed.

9th day: the now initiated offered a libation to the dead from special containers.

10th day: end, return home.

The basis for these mysteries, which were performed from 600 BC to 500 AD, was Demeter's underworld journey, which she undertook to bring back her daughter Persephone/Kore. Demeter's brother Hades had kidnapped her in agreement with Zeus because he wanted her as his wife.

In search of her, Demeter consecrated the boy Triptolemos with fire, i.e. she held him in the hearth fire (gate to the otherworld) of his parents' palace and, had she not been interrupted by Triptolemos' parents, would have conferred immortality on him. She also taught Triptolemos agriculture.

To force Zeus to help her get back her daughter Persephone, Demeter caused a great drought that starved the people. Now that the gods were no longer receiving sacrifices and their worship was no longer being performed, Zeus finally gave in so that Persephone could return.

However, because Persephone had eaten some pomegranate seeds by a trick of Hades, she had to spend a third of the year in the underworld – thus the seasons were created. Persephone returned to the underworld in autumn at the same time when the Mysteries of Eleusis took place. This time fits to the old idea that after the dry summer at this time the weather god brought back the water, i.e. the rain from the giant rain-robber serpernt. After the first rains the grains have been sown.

The return of Demeter and Persephone probably took place (mythologically speaking) on the night of the 8th day of the Mysteries, on the morning of which the priestesses reported their visions and afterwards the Hierophant and the Daduchos sang the songs of praise for Demeter and Persephone. The following feast was also a celebration of the return of Demeter and Persephone from the underworld.

The idea that the gods depended on the offerings of men is also found among the Sumerians and the Celts, among others.

The procedures of the mysteries must have been very effective, because these mysteries were celebrated for about 1,100 years. They were held in high esteem. For example, Plato says of them, "The ultimate purpose of the Mysteries … was to return us to the principles from which we arose … a complete joy in the spiritual good within us."

The Roman orator Cicero also praised the Mysteries of Eleusis: "For among the many excellent, even divine, institutions which your Athens has produced and with which you have enriched human life, nothing is better, in my opinion, than these Mysteries. For by their aid we have been brought out of barbarism and crude life-style and into an educated and refined culture; and the rites are rightly called 'initiations,' for truly: by them we have experienced the beginning of life, and by them we have acquired not only the power to live more happily, but also to die with more hope."

This comment clearly shows that the Mysteries were in large part about the knowledge of one's soul and its destiny after death – and that this destiny of the soul, recognized in the Mysteries, gave new hope to the initiates.

English Books by Harry Eilenstein

- Living Magic (261 p.)
- The Synthesis of Physics and Magic (192 p.)
- Telepathy for Beginners (60 p.)
- Telepathy for Advanced Learners (52 p.)
- Telekinesis for Beginners (56 p.)
- Astral Projection for Beginners (60 p.)
- Meditation for Beginners (60 p.)
- Prophecy for Beginners (60 p.)
- Invocations for Beginners (52 p.)
- Evocations for Beginners (62 p.)
- Auto-Movement for Beginners (60 p.)
- Elves for Beginners (56 p.)
- Hypnosis for Beginners (56 p.)
- Love Magic for Beginners (52 p.)
- Money Magic for Beginners (60 p.)
- Magic Objects for Beginners (64 p.)
- Shamanism for Beginners (52 p.)
- Self Knowledge for Beginners (60 p.)
- Number Symbolism for Beginners (64 p.)

- Ritual Magic for Beginners (64 p.)
- Mandalas for Beginners (76 p.)
- Crop Circles for Beginners (344 p.)
- Feng Shui for Beginners (96 p.)

These books will be puplished soon:

- Life Force for Beginners
- Kundalini for Beginners
- Chakra-Magic for Beginners
- Astrology for Beginners
- Magic Research for Beginners
- Symbolism of Numbers for Beginners
- Language of the Moon – for Beginners
- Magic Chant for Beginners
- Da'ath-Magic for Beginners
- Magic for Beginners – Anthology I
- Magic for Beginners – Anthology II
- Magic for Beginners – Anthology III
- Magic for Beginners – Anthology IV

Bücher von Harry Eilenstein

Religion allgemein
- Die sieben Schritte des Lebens (428 S.)
- Muttergöttin und Schamanen (168 S.)
- Göbekli Tepe (472 S.)
- Die Göttin von Göbekli Tepe (144 S.)
- Totempfähle (440 S.)
- Christus (60 S.)
- Dakini (80 S.)
- Vajra (76 S.)

Ägypten
- Hathor und Re 1: Götter und Mythen im Alten Ägypten (432 S.)
- Hathor und Re 2: Die altägyptische Religion – Ursprünge, Kult und Magie (396 S.)
- Isis (508 S.)

Indogermanen
- Die Entwicklung der indogermanischen Religionen (700 S.)
- Wurzeln und Zweige der indogermanischen Religion (224 S.)

Germanen
- Die Götter der Germanen (87 Bände – siehe nächste Seite)
- Odin (300 S.)

Kelten
- Cernunnos (690 S.)
- Taliesin (228 S.)
- Der Kessel von Gundestrup (220 S.)
- Der Chiemsee-Kessel (76)

Psychologie
- Über die Freude (100 S.)
- Das Geheimnis des inneren Friedens (252 S.)
- Das Beziehungsmandala (52 S.)
- Gefühle und ihre Verwandlungen (404 S.)
- einsgerichtet (140 S.)
- Liebe und Eigenständigkeit (216 S.)
- Von innerer Fülle zu äußerem Gedeihen (52 S.)

Heilung
- Die Symbolik der Krankheiten (76 S.)

Kunst
- Herz des Tanzes – Tanz des Herzens (160 S.)

Drama
- König Athelstan (104 S.)

Bücher von Harry Eilenstein

„Magie für Anfänger"

- Telepathie für Anfänger (60 S.)
- Telepathie für Fortgeschrittene (52 S.)
- Telekinese für Anfänger (52 S.)
- Lebenskraft für Anfänger (60 S.)
- Meditation für Anfänger (56 S.)
- Kundalini für Anfänger (100 S.)
- Hypnose für Anfänger (56 S.)
- Auto-Movement für Anfänger (56 S.)
- Chakra-Magie für Anfänger (148 S.)
- Astralreisen für Anfänger (56 S.)
- Astrologie für Anfänger (120 S.)
- Ritual-Magie für Anfänger (56 S.)
- Mandalas für Anfänger (68 S.)
- Geldzauber für Anfänger (56 S.)
- Liebeszauber für Anfänger (52 S.)
- Invokationen für Anfänger (52 S.)
- Evokationen für Anfänger (60 S.)
- Elfen für Anfänger (56 S.)
- Magie-Forschung für Anfänger (140 S.)
- Selbsterkenntnis für Anfänger (52 S.)
- Zahlensymbolik für Anfänger (60 S.)
- Die Sprache des Mondes – für Anfänger (116 S.)
- Zaubergesänge für Anfänger (100 S.)
- Zukunftschau für Anfänger (60 S.)
- Schamanismus für Anfänger (52 S.)
- Magische Gegenstände für Anfänger (68 S.)
- Da'ath-Magie für Anfänger (64 S.)
- Kornkreise für Anfänger (348 S.)
- Feng Shui für Anfänger (96 S.)
- Magie für Anfänger – Sammelband I (696 S.)
- Magie für Anfänger – Sammelband II (664 S.)
- Magie für Anfänger – Sammelband III (580 S.)

„Traumreisen"

- Traumreisen zu Heilpflanzen (700 S.)

Magie

- Handbuch für Zauberlehrlinge (408 S.)
- Tarot (104 S.)
- Physik und Magie (184 S.)
- Die Synthese von Physik und Magie (200S.)
- Die Magie-Formel (156 S.)
- Krafttiere – Tiergöttinnen – Tiertänze (112 S.)
- Schwitzhütten (524 S.)
- Mythen und Magie der Harfe (116 S.)
- Magie heute – Berichte aus der Praxis (288 S.)

Meditation

- Der Lebenskraftkörper (230 S.)
- Die Chakren (100 S.)
- Das Chakren-System mit den Nebenchakren (296 S.)
- Organe und Chakren (64 S.)
- Die platonischen Körper in den Chakren (156 S.)
- Meditation (140 S.)
- Drachenfeuer (124 S.)
- Kundalini I (676 S.)
- Reinkarnation (156 S.)
- einsgerichtet (140 S.)

Astrologie

- Astrologie (496 S.)
- Photo-Astrologie (428 S.)
- Die astrologischen Aspekte (88 S.)
- Horoskop und Seele (120 S.)

Kabbala

- Kursus der praktischen Kabbala (150 S.)
- Eltern der Erde (450 S.)
- Blüten des Lebensbaumes:
    - Die Struktur des kabbalistischen Lebensbaumes (370 S.)
    - Der kabbalistische Lebensbaum als Forschungshilfsmittel (580 S.)
    - Der kabbalistische Lebensbaum als spirituelle Landkarte (520 S.)

Die Themen der 87 Bände der Reihe „Die Götter der Germanen"